FALSE PROPHETS AND THE PATH OF THE SPIRITUAL WARRIOR

JOHN OFFICER

outskirts
press

Outskirts Press, Inc.
http://www.outskirtspress.com

Paperback ISBN: 978-1-9772-1166-8
Hardback ISBN: 978-1-9772-1167-5

Outskirts Press and the "OP" logo are trademarks belonging to Outskirts Press, Inc.

PRINTED IN THE UNITED STATES OF AMERICA

About the Author

John Officer is a full professor of physical education with tenure at the U.S. Naval Academy. He served as head men's tennis coach at Navy for thirty years before retiring from coaching several years ago. Currently he is director of the USNA Athletic Association Coaches Group. He schedules motivational speakers for the coaches. He has served as a member of the Faculty Senate and is the chair of the Physical Development Committee for the Physical Education Department. He is also chair of the Racquets Electives.

Three years ago he started a scholarship program. He takes one student per year and offers free lessons. The first year the recipient was Alex Cauneac. Alex finished his high school career by winning the Maryland State Singles title defeating the number-three player in the country in the finals. Currently he coaches Jelani Sarr who has reached #2 in country.

As a college coach Officer won more than 450 matches which is the most wins in the history of Navy tennis. He has won ten conference titles, including two in the Colonial Athletic Association and eight in the Patriot League, which is the most of any coach in league history. His seven Patriot League Coach of the Year awards are the most in league history. Coach Officer was voted Intercollegiate Tennis Association Region I Coach of the Year twice. On a national level he was voted

USPTA National Coach of the Year in 1991. Additionally he spoke to the ITA National Convention on four separate occasions. He has spoken to eighteen different sports teams at the Naval Academy. Coach Officer wrote a philosophy book titled "Discovering Your Passion: The Path of the Spiritual Warrior". Also he wrote a cutting-edge tennis book titled "Advanced Stroke Mechanics and Tactics". He produced ten videos on the game of tennis. He was also prolific in writing articles based on research grants. He completed research grants on U.S. tennis, the warrior ethos, Spanish tennis, and Scottish tennis. Finally, Coach Officer has developed a system for teaching stroke mechanics titled Johnny O's Tennis System. His system incorporates seventy-one different shots that are to be mastered for an aspiring pro tour player.

Preface

This book, *False Prophets: The Path of the Spiritual Warrior*, is about a

new-age spiritual warrior ethos. Psychology defined the human mind

as having a logical and a creative component. Psychology is just 150

years old, and I believe it does not have the solutions to human per-

formance. My conclusion is that the mind is made up of a warrior

and a spiritual part of our brain. The warrior side is justice oriented,

tough, relentless, and stoic. The spiritual side is mercy oriented, for-

giving, fun loving, and peaceful. The combination of the warrior and spiritual creates The Path of the Spiritual Warrior. Men throughout

time have had a slight inclination toward the warrior, while the wom-

en have had a slight bent toward the spiritual. True enlightenment

is found when people choose the middle path. The eastern philoso-

phers proclaimed that the middle path has always been the way to

lasting truth. In this book through a series a one-line proclamations I

show the way to societal enlightenment.

False Prophets and
the Path of the Spiritual Warrior

The path of the spiritual warrior represents the new age rebel Jesus.

Warrior side=tough, relentless, unforgiving, and stoic

Spiritual side=forgiving, softer, sensitive, and fun loving

Acupuncture is an eastern practice worthy of our attention.

Can "real" men, do yoga?

Why do women talk so much?

You can attain a spiritual life without religion.

Be ethical in all that you do; have a personal moral code.

Nurture both sides of your mind (spiritual and warrior), creating the middle path.

Ped socks are strictly for girls.

Get off the phone and iPad and find the wonder in life.

Buy a flip phone for calling and texting only.

Do not have internet on your phone; it is simply addictive.

Do something creating value free of charge on a regular basis.

Maintain a stable weight, exercise five days a week, and sleep eight hours.

Believe in others when no one else will.

No behind-the-back correspondence; handle issues face-to-face.

Develop a hobby in retirement.

Take your time, and get it right the first time.

Be fiercely loyal and do the right thing when no one is looking.

There needs to be a twenty-year statute of limitations on adult sexual

harassment claims.

Stand up for what is right. It takes less courage than you would think.

Be skeptical of technology. Easier does not always equate to better.

Stay away from online banking.

Pay bills by check on the first and fifteenth of each month.

Avoid using the word "great." Greatness is bestowed long after the

fact.

Positive and negative are stupid words. They have fourteen definitions.

They mean nothing.

Man and woman is often the perfect union God and Jesus were looking for.

Tony Robbins and Joel Osteen are frauds. Truman did not need their vapid diatribes .

The pillars of the new age movement are Joseph Campbell and Scott Peck.

Dr. Phil gave us the inner child. A "real" man finds this way of thinking meaningless.

Kennedy was an unapologetic womanizer. "Real" men don't trust womanizers.

Jimmy Carter was a true man of God but very weak in leadership skills.

Obama did nothing of significance for eight years and yet had high approval ratings.

We will now put America first.

Any country that harbors terrorists is not allowed entrance to the

USA for one year.

Hollywood is a bastion of liberalism out of touch in la-la land.

Democrats used to be tough under Harry. Now they just whine.

I was raised a democrat, but now I do not recognize the party. I am an

independent.

The flower children destroyed America. They protested all institutions

and did nothing.

Modern fathers are soft and have abdicated their role as head of the

household.

Our children are now overly mothered.

Boston is a tough, honest, and loyal town despite the Catholics.

Boston College is an institution that fosters cocky and ethical leaders.

The Jesuits are generally a complete embarrassment.

Truman was completely ethical. He represents the true balance of the middle path.

Mother Teresa represents the spiritual side of the middle path.

General Patton represents the warrior side of the middle path.

The middle way is the path to true enlightenment.

Be a rigorous follower of **the path of the spiritual warrior.**

Little league games are now filled with wussie fathers yelling at the umpires.

Women are filling the void left by soft men.

Never write in behind a teacher's back.

As a man do not create a friendship with another man's wife.

How can priests parcel out marriage advice, when they have no experience?

Women are constantly pecking at men until the guys simply cave in.

The Jews will be on board when the new age rebel Jesus arrives.

The Germans have never adequately repented for six million Jewish lives.

Equal pay for men and women is obvious.

Psychologists are meant to counsel people who are down on their luck.

Psychiatrists hand out medicine for a balanced life but refuse their

labels.

Play with your grandchildren. Get down on their level.

Know to the penny your daily net worth.

Every man needs a man cave for an office.

Drink single malt scotch on a regular basis with good friends.

Men should smoke a cigar once a week with a friend.

Keep an incredibly clean house.

Whenever possible have someone else mow the grass.

Publish a book on your passion.

Live with your parents or in-laws when possible. They have much wis-

dom to impart.

Be intimidated by no one.

Live a simple life.

Take four weeks off every year to reinvigorate yourself and your family.

Use a handyman when you lack those skills.

Honor thy father and cherish thy mother.

Men never wear a speedo. It is much too effeminate.

Enjoy your high school and college buddies, even if you talk only once

a year.

Dress up for church.

Give your children adequate space.

Go see live music of your choice once a month.

Support your friends when no one else will.

Men need to be kind yet incredibly tough when necessary.

Men and women are fundamentally different. Rejoice in our contradictions.

Get your nose out of your phone. Men and women, pay attention to your spouse instead.

What if God was your janitor?

It is time for a new age bible combining the first two.

Being spiritual is more important than being religious.

Listen twice as much as you speak.

Do not talk over another.

Our daily dialogue needs more significance.

Men, respect strong women. Marriage is a partnership.

Men, do not put your hands on another woman except for a distant hug.

Do not covet another man's wife.

Men, do not call another man's wife. Let the women call each other.

Men and women should be completely professional in the business world.

Business lunches should include groups, not a man and a woman only.

See the good in your family members. Everyone is flawed.

Small daily successes lead to big results.

Dinner table conversation should include children. Do not correct them.

Schools, back your teachers.

The child, when it comes to authority figures, is almost always wrong.

Take a nap once a day.

Walk your dog every day.

Drink for sure, but in moderation.

The flower children loved LSD. Unfortunately it turned them into women.

Men, be stoic, but with a modicum of sensitivity.

Take suicide proclamations seriously.

Write down fifty goals and keep them on your computer.

Depression can come from low goals. Always strive for the top.

Wealthy people should invest in the USA.

Keep one credit card for business and one for the home, but no department store credit cards.

Always pay your credit card bills in full every month.

Check bank statements for complete accuracy.

Men, give your wives a financial report once a month.

Shut down the Catholic Church and give its riches to the less fortunate.

The new age spirituality should be a balance of Harry Truman and

Joseph Campbell.

Harvard is an overrated institution. Go to a school where the faculty

actually teaches.

Hard work should be a given.

When you fall, get right back up every time.

If you need something done quickly, seek out a busy person.

Use sarcasm seldomly and only clearly in good fun.

Be the party house of your neighborhood. Host two large parties per year.

Give to others, even when there is no return effort.

Families should eat dinner together without pointless technological gadgets.

Children should always do their own homework and fill out their own college applications.

Be aggressive in refusing to accept labels.

Watching TV without commercials is preferable.

Expect the best. Do your best, and do not settle for mediocrity.

Bill Belichick is not all that impressed with others, much like our fathers.

Men, develop a relationship with your barber. Go to a regular barber

shop and tip well.

Men, wear new age clothing, not out-of-date preppy clothes.

Women, do not belittle your husbands.

Be loyal to your doctor.

Do not apologize for high standards.

The 1960s was anti-authority. Flower children grew up mistrusting all

institutions.

The 1950s were a good decade with a slight sensitive twist needed for

fathers.

Use no technology devices past six p.m. Never store a cell phone in

the bedroom.

Psychologists tell us that stress can cause mental issues.

The medical research community has one year to find a cure for cancer.

Companies save money by providing only internet solutions to customer issues.

Avoid divorce whenever possible. It ruins families temporarily and sometimes forever.

Men, admit your shortcomings and quietly overcome them.

Do not make the same mistake twice.

Get a writing pad for future correspondence.

Men, take the time to dress like an artist.

People should be constantly evolving.

Drink coffee in moderation every day.

Competition is part of the fun of life and not something to be avoided.

Parents, do not let your children win. It creates a false sense of security.

Play entertaining games with the family once a week.

Do not be in a hurry to get up from the dinner table.

Watch PBS for the nightly news. It is an educated way to become

informed.

Find a funny show, such as *monk,* to watch once a week.

Men, do not shave on the weekends and vacations, but shave for work

every day.

Be an honest straight-up person. Keep no secrets..

People can read through your half truths.

Women, enjoy the silence.

Be true to your word every time.

Take the time to really listen to others.

Young people are simply average. Ask more questions in order to learn

Respect the office of the president, if possible.

Honor the military. They make huge sacrifices on your behalf.

The only thing the flower children got right was that the Vietnam war

was a poor decision.

Be very tough on your child only once for misbehavior.

Grandchildren are a blessing from God.

What about the financial needs of the inner cities?

Boston and San Francisco are the birthplace of the new age movement.

Canadians are very nice neighbors.

Fidelity is a serious matter.

Spain has Gaudi and Barcelona.

Scotland is home to Oban scotch, which is the best in the world.

Young men now keep their hair in a "man bun," which looks hideous.

Holland is full of humble people.

Swedish people are stoic .

My dad wrote nine books without a computer.

Forgiveness is optional.

Terrorists are the true evil enemy.

Australia has the outback and improved wines.

A child must know that his father is truly ethical.

Brazilians hosted the Olympics despite green water.

Ireland has some tough hombres and the cranberries.

Italians have Florence, which simply is the best art city in the world.

Medical experts need to find a cure for schizophrenia immediately!

Jamaica is home to the visionary prophet Bob Marley.

Japan has made amends, unlike Germany.

Kenya is always running from something.

Bosnia has had to deal with cold-blooded Russian aggression.

Cold weather is only slightly tolerable.

Russia turned from a friend in world war ii to our biggest adversary

very quickly.

Keep the innocent child in you alive, in order to see the wonder in life.

Nelson Mandela withstood incredible ignorance.

South Korea tries hard despite a nasty neighbor.

The Wizard of Oz was soft underneath his facade.

Mick Jagger and Stephen Tyler are way too effeminate for "real" men.

The band toad the wet sprocket represents the path of the spiritual

warrior.

Jim Morrison was a new age man.

John and Yoko should have stayed in England.

Why are none of the four Beatles ranked in the top twenty in any

music polls?

Elvis became fat, which was disappointing.

"Real" men love the slide guitar.

Brady and Belichick are the best combination in sports. It is a 1950's type of relationship.

Sports reveal character.

What is a "Hallmark" moment, anyway?

The cell phone is not for vapid texts with a younger woman.

Canadians are tougher than they appear.

The stranger the better for Hollywood.

Goodness is innate. Only psychopaths are evil.

Charles Manson should have been put to death immediately.

Mother Teresa was an absolute saint.

Why did our fathers avoid labels, while today's men gladly oblige?

Attention deficit disorder is a sham.

One bad teacher is not enough reason to doubt the rest.

Billy Clinton did not inhale. What a joke! Everyone inhaled in the 1970s.

Is it too much to ask our leaders to be ethical?

Dredging up dirt on an opponent is what politicians do every day.

The gun lobby fronted by the NRA is totally ignorant.

It should be a challenge for children to surpass their fathers.

Buy American whenever possible.

No one really wants to hear you drone on.

The oldest child has it tougher, but it's not a license to whine.

Get a friend to teach you about the bible.

Discovering your passion: the path of the spiritual warrior is a book for new

agers.

Men, take time to surround yourself with loyal friends.

If there is no father in the home, then find a mentor for your son.

Mistakes are simply part of the learning process.

Momentary issues are not permanent.

Be able to laugh at your mistakes.

Be able to take a stand for what you believe in without alienating others.

It is possible your old technology is still relevant.

Buy two pairs of nice sunglasses in case you lose one.

Men focus on the Old Testament while women follow the New Testament.

Jesus was tougher than depicted and will be even more strident in the second coming.

Jesus was not the complete answer the first time. He is coming back

to judge this time.

Men and women, be devoted to your spouse.

Be clear in your thoughts.

Being organized takes daily attention to the small things.

Never take supplies home from work. Everything starts with minor

indiscretions.

Elizabeth Taylor needed a calculator to keep track of her marriages.

Men, if possible tend to a garden.

Parents, ask your kids to keep their rooms clean and make a proper

bed every day.

Companies need humans who speak English to pick up the phone on the first ring.

"Real" men often do not start things, but they certainly do finish them.

Little kids are often brats, rather than always precious.

The New Age Trinity

God (warrior)

the path of the spiritual warrior featuring the new age

rebel, Jesus,

Replaces the holy spirit (dated)

The middle way is the path to enlightenment, which is the fusion of

the warrior and spiritual

Jesus (spiritual)

The answer to being born again is the path of the spiritual warrior

Pity, oh one of little faith.

Use technology, not the other way around.

Listen to what my followers say about me. (new age Jesus)

"Real" men scaled the beach at Normandy in the direct face of the evil

Germans.

Vietnam was a colossal mistake. Do not ever send our boys to war for

nothing.

George Bush lied just once about the weapons of mass destruction.

The flower children spat on our boys who served with distinction.

Trump can't define the word ethical.

Our country was founded on capitalism. Competition is good.

You are simply a weasel if you go behind someone's back.

Carry yourself with distinction.

Men, maintain a library in your office with special books.

Do not fool with me on ethical issues. You will incur my wrath.

Little girls used to play house. What happened?

Buy a nice house and pay off the mortgage early.

Ali was good but not great.

Jackie O. had grace despite her womanizing husband, who learned

from his dad.

Joseph Kennedy stole elections and was not of Beantown character.

When you are standing on ethical ground you have nothing to fear.

Men, get a dog that will always be loyal to you no matter what.

Forrest Gump was in reality very learned.

Use the word *aplomb*. It is a gentler superlative that means a high

degree of skill.

Do your job with distinction to remain safe.

Sorry to inform you, but your wonder kids are average at best, but

with potential.

"Helicopter" parents are now calling their precious youngsters in col-

lege daily.

Mothers, do not try to be like men. It is unbecoming.

Men, please stop being pansies. Be more like your father.

Esoteric is good word. It means very unusual. Keep a little mystery

about yourself.

Raise the minimum wage to a living wage.

Treat the janitor with the same care as you treat the president.

Are men cowboys and women saints?

Words can hurt.

Do not bury your face in a device in order to run from your shallow life.

Go out to eat once a week for good food. Please look into your spouse's eyes.

Be comfortable being alone for long stretches.

Why does it appear the ERA is still on shaky ground?

The hippies were ultimately soft, but they did help men to be more sensitive.

Avoid car loans.

Black and white pictures have value for an artist.

Local stores are rapidly losing ground to the internet.

Small towns used to be devoid of fast food restaurants.

Take time with all the people who cross your path.

Keep learning.

Williams is a better school than Harvard.

Boston college would be the best school in the country if not for the

Jesuits.

Manage yourself, regardless of any medicine. Medicine is only a piece

of wholeness.

The mental professions often keep people down with labels rather

than lift them up.

What happened to the word *pinhead?*

In the old days not everyone necessarily played. If you were bad you rode the bench.

Boys and girls need to learn early that you do not get something for

nothing.

Equal playing time for youth sports is a form of socialism.

Ignore your child once in a while.

Always be appropriate in your relations with the opposite sex.

A friend who does not speak well of you behind your back is no friend

at all.

How come only Boston people say "wicked pissa?"

Terrorists are pure unadulterated evil, finally a conflict America can get

behind.

Crush your enemies completely.

There should be no more altar boys.

Classical music is akin to getting a root canal. The 1970s music is the best!

The 1950s were dominated by Elvis and Frank.

Tick someone off once a day.

A man cave is better with a window.

Live with one of your parents but maintain a high-quality private social life.

Why do our companies get rid of middle managers and their corporate knowledge?

Why do we have a presidents day when so many are unethical?

Companies, take pride in retaining your people.

Take extra care of West Virginia, the inner cities, and the rust belt.

Everyone is whining about keeping terrorists out. Did we forget internment camps?

Have a copy of the daily newspaper delivered, rather than read the news from an iPod.

Can a conservative really define the word *liberal*?

Trickie Dick ran out of tricks.

Led Zeppelin, by the ratings, is the best band ever.

Money must be earned.

Alexander Hamilton was the founder of capitalism.

Starbucks is ridiculous. Tall is small; grande is medium; venti is large.

What a joke!

Telling your children they are great while yet untested is a recipe for

mediocrity.

Was Gerald Ford really that ignorant?

The space race was fueled by egos.

Greed will catch up to you.

Do not be beholden to computer gadgets.

If you have not failed you have not tried.

Walk tall.

The police are mostly good with a few glaring exceptions.

Who is the woman speaking to us on MapQuest?

Asking good questions is the defining characteristic of a good person.

Have you noticed millenials do not ask questions?

Weak and timid men lack moral fiber.

If it is worth doing, it is worth doing right.

"I told you so." (1950s father speak)

Satan is in the details of temptation.

Mary Tyler Moore was engaging and fun and represented single woman

well.

"This is going to hurt me more than it hurts you." (1950s father speak)

Fortunately we are beyond fish sticks on Fridays for Catholics.

James Carville and Mary Matalin show us that liberals and conserva-

tives can get along.

Why did our moms give us chicken soup on sick days?

Take on projects at work without being asked.

Leave your religious beliefs at home. Work is about inclusiveness.

Do not settle.

Pet rock?

"I need to cajole my lazy son/daughter to do anything." This is a helicopter parent.

Fathers should be vociferous in laying down the law in the household.

What are 1,000 points of light?

Trump uses instagram like a twelve-year-old.

Handle sensitive issues face to face rather than via email.

National healthcare should be a right.

Why is it so hard to collect the money we are owed from internet purchases unwanted?

The healthcare issue prevents workers from taking chances.

The word *positive* is vague and overused.

Morals have been replaced personal values.

Whatever happened to the saying, "I've got your back?"

Companies need to be forced to stop sending unwanted generic emails.

Early risers make significantly more money.

We should send our children to war only in order to win.

Traveling on a cruise ship is no vacation at all.

I hope someone made a lot of money from sticky notes.

Having weddings in churches is not in vogue with the millenials.

Is Andy Warhol's portfolio really art?

Jim Croce and Vincent van Gogh became famous only after their deaths.

Try talking to your dentist while he works on your teeth.

As parents we often teach our children they are the center of the universe.

My prep school teacher was known for his caustic iterations.

The supreme court is only for ethical nonpartisan judges.

O. J. Was guilty.

Large families avoid the mistake of parental overattention with children.

It is not necessary to know every detail of your child's college experience.

The Titanic cleaved into an iceberg, thus ending the brief life of the unsinkable ship.

If you are picked last for pickup basketball, try the piano.

My Dad came to my college only to see me graduate. I turned out ok.

Gym teachers can no longer pick sides for sports. It hurts their students' self-esteem.

The flower children's style of parenting includes mindless adulation.

Respect all people. Everyone is good at something.

Nancy Reagan was overindulgent with cowboy Ronnie .

Learn to compete by playing to win with your brothers. Give them nothing free.

The desolate town of Youngstown lost the tire business it so richly counted on.

Set performance as well as results goals. Performance goals relate to the process.

By age eighteen your precious children are adults. Their decisions are their own.

Technology has exacted a high price on a gullible populace.

The turn-of-the-century wealthy aristocrats eventually got hit with taxes.

Two-year mandatory military service is common in most countries.

Trump is devoid of morals.

Men need to pick out their own clothes.

Country clubs are for those who are insecure.

It is human nature for fathers to be stoic.

It is human nature for mothers to nurture.

Scott peck's new age book, *The Road Less Traveled*, woke up the flower children.

Jesus counted on his progeny to speak the word to the masses.

Al Capone embezzled funds from the city of Chicago without remorse.

Washington gadflies are in gridlock, not understanding the art of compromise.

Today's college students lack the internal fortitude to act independently.

The soft computer generation is in constant gamification mode.

Scientists can be brutal with each other.

A pinhead is one who lacks social graces.

It is ok for women to clip men's ear hairs?

When I was a child we remained at the dinner table until everyone was finished.

Men do not wear winter knit hats with a pom-pom on top.

Facebook is for women and girls only.

Twitter is an opportunity to make inappropriate retorts. Just ask Trump.

Why do twenty-five to forty-year olds not ask questions?

All college graduates begin their careers as "mediocre." Time will tell.

Fathers need to use their dads as an example. Be tough and stoic and

yet still spiritual.

Is $400,000 not enough to get another Harry Truman as president?

Pedicures might be ok for men.

Be proud of the length of your marriage. Love should continue to grow

over time.

Wearing sneakers to work is inappropriate for men.

Mental issues are absolutely not excuses for poor performance.

College professors are supposed to teach undergraduates, not focus

on research.

Gaudi was an incredible genius who went about his life's work ex-

tremely deliberately.

Motorcycles are simply dangerous. Just ask Duane Allman.

Bose is still the best speaker company in the world.

Be kind to everyone you meet. You don't know when you will walk in

their shoes.

"Go outside and get out of my hair," said the 1950s mother to her

nuisance son.

In the 1960s, why did girls have to learn piano while boys played sports?

Big families are things of the past. You got ignored and had to figure things out .

Today's families have one or two children with an overabundance of

attention placed on each.

Why do so many politicians avoid military service?

Teal is a good color because it is a synthesis of other colors. The mid-

dle path is best.

Maker's Mark is the best bourbon.

The millenials need to realize you simply don't get the finer things in

life right away.

Parents should never live vicariously through their children.

When you are working on your passion, the time drifts by quickly.

The Doors were a group of incredibly bright and yet eccentric individuals.

Axel Rose of Guns and Roses is a warrior, even though he disguises

himself as a punk

Joe Montana said fear of failure was his biggest motivator.

Why does Hollywood place Freddie Mercury on a pedestal?

How did we end up with two bands named the who and the guess

who?

The dog show is strictly for girls.

Pit bulls are nasty and belong in a caged environment.

Avoid buying a home of the cookie-cutter variety.

Keep zero credit card debt. Pay your credit card bill off in full every

month.

Attain a retirement specialist to invest your money for the long term.

It is healthier to exercise outdoors.

Retain the quarterly statements of your investments. Keep it on

Quicken.

Have manila folders in your filing cabinet with typed labels. Update

quarterly.

Brush your teeth twice a day.

Be kind to your service people. They may be judging you in heaven.

Learn about the janitor who services your office. Take the time to

know about his or her life.

Inauthentic people are the bane of our existence.

One true friend is better than five fake ones.

As a dad do not blame teachers. Your child is generally in the wrong.

An honest conversation involves give and take, rather than one-way

traffic.

Don't deal in rumors.

Martin Luther King, Jr., was inspirational with a life cut short.

Branch Dravidians were incredibly ignorant and followed a false profit.

The second coming will be led by the rebel Jesus. It is not about mira-

cles but clear insights.

Forgiveness without repentance is pointless.

War is relevant as long as we have clear evil to fight.

Women have filled the void left by weak men.

Girls tend to look to their father's example for a marriage partner.

Amazon will soon replace loyal hard-working people.

Singles bars are a cesspool of losers.

How do you find a soulmate? You sense something right away.

Give your hired help a healthy bonus for Christmas.

Gender has nothing to do with who is more qualified.

Words are the measure of a person.

The young are not the equals or friends of their parents.

Earn your way. Absolutely get rid of participation trophies. They mean

nothing.

If children have subpar skills, they should sit the bench until they

improve.

Tom Brady was a reserve at Michigan who now has won six super bowls. Believe.

Sports are competitive. You either strive to be the best or find another passion.

Learning to win is the first step.

Snow is charming and annoying at the same time.

Why is right field the resting place for those who can't get it done?

Men, if outsiders disparage your family, cross them off the list.

Any changes in life should be made with care.

Mistakes have consequences but are also key learning experiences.

Excuses are simply reasons to fail.

Strive to be the best at what you do.

Canada has a little boy as prime minister.

Forgiveness is optional. Egregious actions warrant crossing people off your list.

Harry dropped the bomb on the japs and slept that night.

Gomer Pyle was smarter than we knew.

Laughter is contagious as long it's not at another person's expense.

Try not to be too sensitive.

I will tell you something one time.

Why is the TV family hour no longer focused on good values?

Haight-Ashbury was for drugged-out flower children who hated authority.

Viagra is an expensive way to please the wife.

Men, join a book club too.

Those fancy soft leather shoes with a buckle are for metrosexual guys.

Charles Manson is a compelling enough reason for the death penalty.

Men should play pebble beach once.

Golf takes the athletic skill of monopoly.

Smoke a cigar while playing golf. It dulls the pain.

Maintain the same local staple of stores regardless of price.

"Real" men drink single-malt scotch.

Father, your children should do it because you said so. End of story.

Men, really scare your children just once.

Prodding children is the mantra of flower children, simply a failed

concept.

Your children should respect you simply because you are the parent.

Live in a balanced climate exposing you to the full range of the seasons.

Fathers should be true warriors and mothers unequivocal saints.

Jesus is among us. Judgment day is upon us. Atheists get on the bus before it is too late.

Act like your accomplishments are no big deal unless challenged.

Unconditional love includes letting go when appropriate.

Drink together at family reunions but do not make a fool of yourself.

The older brother has it harder. Be there for him as he deals with expectations.

Grandchildren are precious for sure, but they also go home at the end of the day.

How come no one wears dickies anymore?

Do you remember the first time you wet your pants?

Fathers, teach your sons masculine principles.

Play intensely with your grandkids for twenty minutes, and then read

the newspaper.

No one is great except harry Truman and God.

Name your children basic, understandable names.

Be proud; have an ego the size of Montana, but at a moment's notice

be humble.

The slide guitar is a metaphor for life thanks to Duane Allman.

Take in a concert every once in a while.

Why is Jimi Hendrix rated ahead of Stevie Ray Vaughn as a guitarist?

Seek knowledge by yourself. Do not rely on the rumor mill.

America is the promised land. Period.

Refuse to order Starbucks using its nomenclature. This is America,

buddy!

Insurance is only for things you can't replace.

There is always one family member who holds up the dinner hour

because of slow eating.

Highly ethical people shy away from congress.

The flower children have grown up to be against all authority.

The silly word *positive* has fourteen definitions in the dictionary. It is

vague.

Lotharios are the bane of a loyal tough guy's existence.

The expression on the faceless son was placid in his approach to motivation.

People who cliff jump are taking fearlessness to a new insanity.

America should be a country of moral principles, not vapid values.

Respect your father and do not denigrate him.

Keep a day timer for appointments not your laptop.

Avoid the internet. It is addictive.

Be generous when tipping.

Every good band has at least three hits.

Coconut cake is special.

Belichick and his father were both curmudgeons.

Why do professional leagues name an MVP before the championship?

The internet comes at a cost.

When you say you will do something, do it right away.

Medical expenses prevent talented people from considering entrepreneurship.

Divorce initiated by a man is often explained as a midlife crisis.

Pay for a good accountant. It beats being audited.

The young worker has made a slew of mistakes. Certain mistakes are part of the process.

Drive slowly. What is the hurry? Besides, you have satellite radio.

The corporate tax rate needs to be 20%. Trust the extra money will go to the people.

Go to bank tellers. Know them by name. Do not use ATM machines.

The cloud is risky. Keep control of everything .

Collect cool blazers and shirts from a consignment shop nearby.

Be afraid of absolutely no one but take into accounting of their criticisms too.

Use a flip phone for calls and texting only. Are the barrage of pictures all that important?

Get angry over ethical issues only. The rest is wasteful.

In past days it took only one tongue lashing for the little brat to get the message.

How come every woman now wears fancy boots?

It now takes a female blond to ascertain the weather.

The flower children say God is a woman. Seriously?

Small business is the foundation of capitalism.

Let women drive. They are more logical.

Frisbees were invented by flower children who got tired of playing

right field.

Savor your food.

Men wear slightly feminine clothing as metrosexuals.

What did we learn about finances from playing monopoly?

"Damn it," barked the 1950's dad.

Cars are disposable. Hold onto to them.

Dare to "travel to the beat of different drum."

Read Scott Peck and Joseph Campbell.

Our military is ready to respond to evil.

A father should never be obsequious toward his children.

The Myers Briggs personality test was the only psychological tool worth anything.

Rest on Sundays.

The grateful dead are washed up flower children.

We all need a computer person to make sense of the expansive internet.

Laugh and love often.

United nations: if you want to play ball, then pay up!

When men take charge, women relax.

"A quitter never wins, and a winner never quits."

The 1970s showcased terrific bands still going strong.

Allow our elderly to age gracefully. They have earned it.

Disco promoted promiscuous behavior.

Captain kangaroo was fat and too effeminate.

Alexander Hamilton founded capitalism as we know it.

Mister Rogers was a pathetic role model for young boys.

No guy should say "yummy."

The 1950s was a wonderful decade but devoid of sensitivity for the coming new-age man.

1990s music rebounded from the 80's.

Where did the word *creep* go?

Fly fishing has a high failure rate and is not for the faint of heart.

Y2K was a fiasco leaving people wondering if this was the second coming. Not yet!

Our kids know they are not great, regardless of our pontificating.

The kid with the coke-bottle glasses was ungainly on the basketball court.

Jesus was at times effeminate, except when exploding on those who sought commerce.

The Monkees had a career in music as pseudo talents, albeit briefly.

Maine people describe newcomers as "from away."

What is all the hoopla over rap music with its pathetic, demeaning lyrics?

The flower children drifted through the 1960s with a laissez-faire attitude.

Introverts do not get their energy from dealing with others.

Amazon was the idea of Jeff Bezos, and now they won't pick up the phone.

How many times did you throw up after drinking Boone's farm wine in high school?

" know the end is coming soon. Rebel Jesus.

Father knows best was replaced by a pathetic version of dad.

Four dead in Ohio.

Everyone should read *The Power of the Myth* by Joseph Campbell.

Let's not forget about the Old Testament.

Snowball pastries were tasty, but why pink?

Joseph Kennedy was afraid to take on the Nazis.

George Wallace was liked only by Lynyrd Skynyrd and a few rednecks..

When confronted with clear unethical behavior, cross the person off

your list.

I boycott visiting Germany. Six million Jews were exterminated. Enough

said.

"I am not of this world." (Rebel Jesus)

Trust is a joke today's world.

The Rebel Jesus is God's own messenger.

Why is twenty-seven the age many of the most talented rock stars

pass away?

I don't have time to hear your whine.

Do not share your goals, because others will try to poke holes in your

dreams.

See your dermatologist and eye doctor on a regular basis.

Stay calm under pressure.

When you love what you do, work is more pleasurable.

Devise a plan for semi-retirement.

Eating out should be a treat.

Make a list of stores from which you need their products and remain

loyal. Forget price.

Drink a protein shake every morning.

Life throws you curve balls. Stay the course.

Depression is the new common cold. Take the medications and set higher

goals.

Parents, do not let the medical community impose labels on your children.

Do I really care what someone on Facebook had for breakfast?

A real book is preferable to reading off an iPad.

Question what others do not.

Allow random thoughts to pass by without judging.

The warrior side seeks judgment, while the spiritual side seeks peace.

Prayer is a way to gain enlightenment.

Excess warrior ethos equals a stern view, and too much spirituality makes you meek.

If possible live near the water. It has a calming effect.

Recreational vehicles are not only for rednecks.

Do away with chain stores.

The Wal-Mart company pays employees pennies while its owners all have billions.

Do away with generic mindless houses in copycat neighborhoods .

Boarding school does not allow "helicopter" parents enough time to meddle.

Should parents know what you did as a college student on a particular Friday night?

The New Testament weighs in on the feminine side.

Be patient and give unconditional love to stepchildren.

Freeways are dangerous and inhumane; take side roads whenever possible.

The Wizard of Oz was a tough guy only when hiding behind the curtain.

The Tin Man and the Cowardly Lion were extremely effeminate. What

does this say?

Life can come full circle when we learn from our mistakes.

All is well that ends with moral certitude.

The smallest compliment goes a long way.

Love does not need empty platitudes to endure.

Men, take out the garbage.

Men should find an excuse to bond with other guys—sports, coffee,

drinks, or cards.

Hollywood has proven the ability to make movies without violence

and sex.

Hallmark movies are awesome!

Wooden boats are a sign of class.

The Beatles are for screaming schoolgirls only.

Tea time is only for the ladies.

Everything happens for a reason. (Mom)

The key to financial success: use other people's money. (Dad)

Let's get back to basics, where women cook and men do the dishes.

Why is it that even with all of the technological advances we still get

awful cell service?

All guns should be against the law except pistols and hunting rifles.

Fathers used to point their index fingers for emphasis.

Be careful when using sarcasm.

Divorce is an abject failure. No sugar coating it.

Weather people have a worse batting average than baseball players.

The new legal jargon is guilty, and then you must spend your family fortune in defense.

How do you prove consensual sex?

Do we really believe a person is incapable of change?

A good sermon invokes the old and new testament teachings.

Right-wing zealots take positions counter to common sense.

Is it possible to converse about politics without getting personal?

The cost to my children concerning divorce is palpable.

Men need to own up to their failures with a sense of toughness.

Wear funny-colored socks.

The race to the finish concerns judgment day.

The second coming with the Rebel Jesus will preach on love as well

as harsh judgment.

The immoral Jim jones took advantage of innocent people in the name

of God .

Bill Moyer is the best storyteller. The interview with joseph Campbell

was epic.

Men, make daily to-do lists in a daytimer. Women can keep it on their

phones.

Men should hang achievements on the wall in their cave.

Women should come forward immediately concerning abuse without

waiting years.

Women should not wear suggestive clothing.

Porches are not just for the people of Minnesota defending against giant mosquitos.

The new age Rebel Jesus will appear as a prophet during the second coming.

It is unbecoming for artists to support the NRA.

Country music has taken God into the mainstream .

Men should hang a picture of the old family homestead in their cave.

Parents, remain in your original home whenever possible.

Secrets have no place in a healthy marriage.

Why are we the only industrial nation without strict gun laws?

All people need to have a vocabulary calendar. Words are crucial.

What was life like without attention deficit disorder?

Weak psychiatrists gave us the words *manic-depressive*. Thanks so much.

After we rid ourselves of all medical labels, keep the medicine for balance.

Elvis was a prophet who ate one too many hamburgers.

Marilyn was an abused starlet who paid a heavy price for allowing JFK to seduce her.

Only a Kennedy could not stay faithful to Jackie.

When people cross the line either confront them or cross them off the list.

Either get a college degree or work with your hands.

Keep a nice box on your desk of interesting trinkets of significance.

Society will need to get rid of instagram, twitter, and iPads to survive.

We now have husbands and wives with their faces in their devices over

dinner.

Men need only a desktop computer at home and work as well as a flip

phone with no internet.

Laugh off mistakes.

Write handwritten thank you notes.

Writing is the gateway to heaven.

Attain a writing notebook. Write thoughts for emails and only then

pen an email.

Email is acceptable, but use only a few words. Save the rest for face-

to-face contact.

Slow down whenever you are responding to an email.

Do not be a weasel backstabber.

Boys play cowboys and girls play Barbie. Natural instincts?

Lucky charms were a special treat as a kid..

The dirtball who tried to end the wonderful gabby Gifford's life will

pay.

Cubicles are inhumane and lack trust in your employees.

Every man needs an ottoman.

We bury our heads in shame with our iPhones serving as false prophets.

Parental heirlooms handed down are to be professionally refurbished.

Do business locally whenever possible.

Jane Pauley has dealt with her medical condition gracefully.

Guys hugging guys is now acceptable.

Money isn't everything, but it sure is nice.

Regardless of your position in life, carry yourself with strength.

The new metro look for men is slightly effeminate.

Call your sister every week. Call your brother quarterly.

Go-carts were a way for young boys to emulate James dean.

Why is milk not still in bottles and delivered to the door?

Any thoughts on why men are such wussies up against their towering

fathers?

Men, put up many family pictures in your man cave.

Your medical history is absolutely no one's business.

Educated people love 1970s music.

Avoid psycho thrillers. They are bad for the soul.

Most men are the perpetrators of mid-life affairs that cause divorce.

Why do woman at times take cheating husbands back?

People need to fully repent to God for their sins, or there is no forgiveness.

When you wrong another, they may never forgive you.

Give credit where credit is due.

Do not micromanage your children. Soon they will be on their own.

You get what you pay for. Buy one nice purchase rather than three cheap

ones.

Las Vegas is called sin city, clandestine affairs at the cost of the wife.

Gambling is pathetic.

It is time for Bill Gates and Jeff Bezos to give back to America and our

homeless.

We avoid the homeless condition by the grace of God.

The Ed Sullivan show was an important venue for 1960s bands.

If you are fully prepared you will not feel pressure.

Men, wear a bracelet on your wrist and a Celtic cross around your neck for symbolic value.

A simple compliment goes a long way. Regularly write notes of encouragement.

On Saturday night dress up and go out on the town with your spouse or significant other.

Security systems are useless. Lock your doors and trust the Lord instead.

National health care makes sense. Just ask any other country.

Bill Clinton's mother took his underwear to the dry cleaner. Really?

Men with the inability to stay focused should read short stories.

Men should wear a funky neck scarf in the winter. It's metro.

Discovering your passion is the key to sustained excellence.

Adamantly refuse to let the devil take your soul.

Just pick up the telephone. Voice mail is cowardly and impolite.

Use the "index your passion" exercise to uncover dormant interests.

The middle level are agnostics. These people are worth saving.

Psychopaths are evil and not worth saving.

Better late than never. Come to Jesus now or face the consequences.

Respect everyone but fear no one.

Psychiatry: Weyer founded it in 1560. Now psychiatrists simply give out

labels and drugs.

Psychology: James founded it in 1870. Freud is utter crap

Men and women can't be friends. Plain and simple.

One must combine a healthy fear (old testament) with unconditional

love (new testament).

Men who abuse women are psychopaths who do not understand right

from wrong.

You can find all the pertinent facts on writing starting with the dictionary.

The sandwich theory still holds true: compliment, criticism, compliment.

Jews say Jesus was not a prophet; focus is on God. For them, Jesus has

yet to come.

Learn from every situation.

Be intimidated by no one except God.

We know full well when we have been unethical with another. Repent!

Teach your children well on the subject of ethics. (personal moral

code)

Values are simply social norms. They are only what society deems

appropriate.

The rebel Jesus is when Jesus and God will truly become one.

The middle path is the key to a relationship with the new age rebel

Jesus.

Tiny Tim showed overly effeminate tendencies while he "tiptoed

through the tulips."

Dog is a man's best friend as long as he obeys.

The fear of God is the beginning of wisdom.

Doctors administer an onslaught of drugs to their pliable patients.

Men must rise at 6:00 a.m. and retire at 10:00 p.m. use extra time for

spiritual endeavors.

Socialize outside of work.

Let your dog lick your face five minutes a day. It is cathartic.

Regularly drink kombucha. It is good for the intestines.

Why take a chance? Because without taking chances we are not fully

alive.

Give and you shall receive.

Clean up your own mess. (Mom)

I will tell you this just once. (Dad)

When you are in the zone, go with it.

Bob Newhart's answer to psychobabble is two words: "stop it."

Just let things be rather than make things happen" was the flower child

mantra.

You must be joking! (1960s jargon)

The mothers' maudlin musings to her daughter fell on barren ground.

Be still in the midst of turmoil.

Woman have the heart of a child.

Take life inch by inch.

Men, avoid superlatives such as the word "fantastic."

My college girlfriend jilted me for a weasel dickie-wearing Harvard guy.

The Rebel Jesus is tough when necessary and compassionate as needed.

The Beatles were a marketing blitz.

Tom Brady uses fear as a motivator.

Trust is earned.

Give twenty-dollar bills to homeless people at random and for no apparent reason.

Trump is often sophomoric with his tweets.

Music is good for the soul.

Unethical behavior is simply verboten on the path of the spiritual warrior.

Alabama is home to the crimson tide, George Wallace, and Ronnie van Zant.

Alaska has long summer days, huge bears, and Denali for crazy climbers.

Everyone gets a dry mouth in Arizona.

Clinton balanced the budget while managing to court a girl half his age.

California is home to the pathetic flower children who tried to bring down society.

Colorado has lots of pot. It is immature to smoke pot as an adult.

No jail terms for drugs. Punish the dealers, though.

Global warming is real. Ask any of the leading scientists in the world.

Connecticut is super preppy.

The worst thing in school used to be getting the nods in class.

The crossroads are where the spiritual and the warrior intersect.

Delaware is home to the Duponts, wonderful gardens, and very old money.

Florida is the sunshine state inundated with tax dodgers.

There is no reason for you to hide. Walk upright.

Donald Trump is very shaky on the subject of abuse of females.

There were three rules when I was a child: be on time, eat your food, and no whining.

Have a good tech-support person.

Does Verizon ever pick up the phone?

Trump is on twitter as much as a child.

The therapist says to the husband and wife, "Do you two actually talk?"

"Are you big timing me?" asked the coach to the player.

Golf is for logical pinheads, not for creative rebels.

You've got to make it while you can. (on the subject of money).

You may take an unethical stance toward me, but I will get the last

laugh.

It is generally the best policy to inundate others with kindness unless

they cross a line.

People are enamored with other people's issues while their own stare

back at them.

Brace yourself now. (judgment day)

The metro man's accoutrements are now being emulated by many.

If you don't know your history, you are bound to repeat it.

You snooze, you lose. Take action as appropriate.

Build a fire. It is cathartic.

It is not fair for those who seek entry to the U.S. to become citizens.

Hawaii, despite the beauty, is home to the cowardly act perpetrated

by Japan.

We need an independent president to break up the logjam in

congress.

Illinois celebrated the unethical al Capone. Why?

Democrats used to be conservative. (Truman)

Iowa is a political force.

The shutdown was immoral.

Men, stay away from interior decorating. It is strictly for women.

Can an open mind and toughness coexist?

Maine people simply do not much like other people. You have to be born there.

Can a real man use a night light?

Driving in Boston gives you an idea of why Massachusetts people are called crazy.

Serve others, not the other way around.

Slow down and appreciate life.

Jackson is the epitome of a southern town in beautiful Mississippi, despite it's past history.

Harry the haberdasher turned out to be one our best presidents.

Fly fishing takes the patience of job, and east coast people simply are too restless.

Nebraska is home to the cornhusker. What is that?

Play is the highest form of research.

New Hampshire is the granite state with the motto "live free or die."

They mean it!

New jersey is called the garden state, but the turnpike is hardly a garden party.

World war ii featured men who climbed the cliffs of Normandy and lived to tell it.

New Yorkers work harder than anyone but are equally adept at being obnoxious.

North Carolina is home to the tar heel. What the heck is a tarheel?

Men, play golf with friends weekly, just as long as you can remain sane.

Ohio is home to the Kent state massacre. It was a disgraceful act by

the Ohio national guard.

Where does the term *redneck* derive from?

Oregon has the most pot. Is this where the flower children went?

Go on Facebook just once a year to see how many people wished you

happy birthday.

Rhode island is home to the Vanderbilits, as they enjoyed no taxation.

Men, make the bed well every day.

Pay for household services whenever possible.

Tennessee is home to Memphis and the wonderful music on Beale

Street.

Utah has the Mormons and polygamy, which is not biblical.

Texas is home to the musical cowboy Delbert McClinton.

Vermont is home to Ben and Jerry's and a state full of misguided hippies.

The fact that Charlottesville hosted the white racists does not spoil a

great city.

West Virginia has not received any help from Bill Gates.

Billy Clinton says he "did not have sex with that woman." are we that

stupid?

Whatever happened to the word "swell?"

Whatever happened to the saying "atta boy?"

You get what you pay for. Buy local, pay more, purchase less.

Life is like a fine wine; if attended to properly, it ages gracefully.

Men prefer understated clothing for their wives.

No shaving for men on the weekends.

It is time to bring back fedoras.

The coach chastised his guard after he missed a layup, risking being

called "negative."

The Turtles Band had an ephemeral career with only "Happy Together"

to show as a hit.

The flotilla of German U-boats presented an ominous presence off the

U.S. shore.

The ensign had a yen for life at sea.

Real beauty is always natural.

Have we forgotten Bill Russell's eleven championships?

The new age Rebel Jesus is in his incipient second phase here on earth.

You get twenty-four hours to return correspondence. Period.

The 50% divorce rate is mostly about the small things. Say nice things

about your spouse.

Live with family members whenever possible.

Our fathers never told us we were great, and we came out just fine.

Great is a term used long after the fact. It implies we have nothing left

to learn.

A punk is a youth who disrespects his elders.

Everyone is capable of change except psychopaths.

Use words that have clear meanings.

Self-esteem is a term invented by psychologists only recently. Unneces-

sary psychobabble.

Short cuts are unacceptable in business.

Take chances, but never be reckless.

Fear is the ultimate motivator.

Everyone getting a trophy is akin to socialism.

Live life on a deadline.

Is beekeeping really a hobby?

Why don't we hear of sexual advances perpetrated by woman on men?

Don't walk in your loafers.

Promise your mother you will be kind.

When father is in his man cave don't bother him.

Women have learned to be warriors, yet men have become overly soft.

Why do people confuse values and ethics?

When the Rebel Jesus arrives, a new epoch will begin.

A Bose cd player works well in the man cave.

Have a healthy mistrust of technology.

The internet was intended to be addictive.

Allen Collins is the least appreciated great guitarist.

Insist on a heavy-duty flip phone. What everyone is doing is not always the right thing.

Take time when constructing your man cave.

Father "mostly" knows best.

A man should wear a gold watch with a flexible band. It is more manly.

Publish a book concerning your passion.

Why do companies insist on not having an actual person answer the phone?

Bullying is perpetrated by oversized losers with no future.

Fathers should be stoic at little league games.

Fathers should not overly praise their children. There is always room for improvement.

Agnostics are simply unsure.

Atheists are often stubborn and clearly have missed the boat.

Educators need to have very high standards despite enduring the word *negative*.

Your child will eventually fly from the nest. As a parent, hold on loosely.

Do parents think they are fooling colleges when they fill out admissions packages?

Impose an ethical foundation upon your children, but remember it is still their life.

What was so wrong about children playing outside until the dinner bell rang?

Choose an oil painting of significance to you and place it in your man cave.

Check out TV ads lately. Men are depicted as buffoons. It breaks down the father's role.

Men need to refuse to adopt a woman's perspective. Be a man.

The main role of the warrior father is to protect the family.

What does the word *ethics* mean? It is a personal moral code.

A symbolic grandfather clock is a must for the homestead.

Life is what happens while you are on Facebook.

Teachers are not defended by gutless administrators who cave in to parents.

What other job requires you to start at 7:30 a.m. and finish at 10:00 p.m. at night like teachers?

Whatever happened to the teacher's word being paramount?

The words "wait until your father comes home" used to invoke a strong degree of fear.

Is it a good thing that the father figure is now soft and indecisive?

Children should walk a fine line between joking around and respect with Dad.

A mother's default mode is to nurture, while for men it is to instill ethics.

Have your first beer sitting in dad's lap. Learn to drink at home.

Getting even is when your college steady who dumped you married a bald accountant.

If you insist on the path of divorce, make sure it is for your soulmate.

Office parties are treacherous ground. Keep your hands to yourself and limit alcohol.

Women, keep the social calendar.

Keep a bill holder on your desk. Date each bill as to when it is to be paid.

Old-fashioned balancing of the checkbook to the penny is still prudent.

Throw away second-place trophies. They are a sign of mediocrity.

Why does mediation in divorce proceedings rarely work?

Ultimate power corrupts ultimately.

It is unfair to lump all priests together. The Catholics, though, are ab-

solutely wrong.

Why are the major drug companies not held accountable for dumping

opioids?

Why as a country are we inundated with galactic movies?

I was taught by my mother that all people truly are created equal.

Silence is an act of sacredness, but our societal problem is that many

never stop talking.

Whatever happened to a civil discourse between two people?

Trump casts aspersions often.

Sarcasm and sensitivity in men do not go together well.

The immediate nature of our cell phones makes us often reactive.

We have friends for season, reason, and forever.

Get to know your bank teller, avoid using the ATM machine.

Be excellent in all that you do. It is just as easy to do something well

as it is to do it poorly.

The mantra today for a father's discourse with their children is now

vapid superlatives.

It is mindless to move to a state simply because of taxes. Quality of life

is more important.

Why is getting a license renewed such an onerous task?

Dating websites can uncover soulmates as well as psychopaths.

A true artist insists on full control.

How do marriages keep the flame alive when Facebook is a higher

priority?

Women at times talk too much and men do not listen enough.

Evil is alive and well. Be on-guard.

Atheists have no faith but will be given one more chance when the

Rebel Jesus arrives.

Make sure your passion in life is an ethical pursuit.

Avoid looking like everyone else.

This current generation has made working at home fashionable.

It is easier to reel in a rebel than to prod a pansy.

CPSIA information can be obtained
at www.ICGtesting.com
Printed in the USA
BVHW040753260719
554364BV00024B/243/P

9 781977 211675